Part 2
14 more Animals in the Quran
Activity & Coloring Book

By Halimah Bashir
Art by Laila Ramadhani

California, USA
www.prolancewriting.com
© 2025 Halimah Bashir
ISBN: 979-8-9988955-5-5
All rights reserved. No part of the publication may be reproduced in any form without prior permission from the publisher.

Spot the differences

*Goats are excellent climbers and can scale steep terrain; some can even climb trees.

How to draw a Locust

*Locusts can form massive swarms that travel great distances; some swarms contain billions of insects and cover hundreds of square miles.

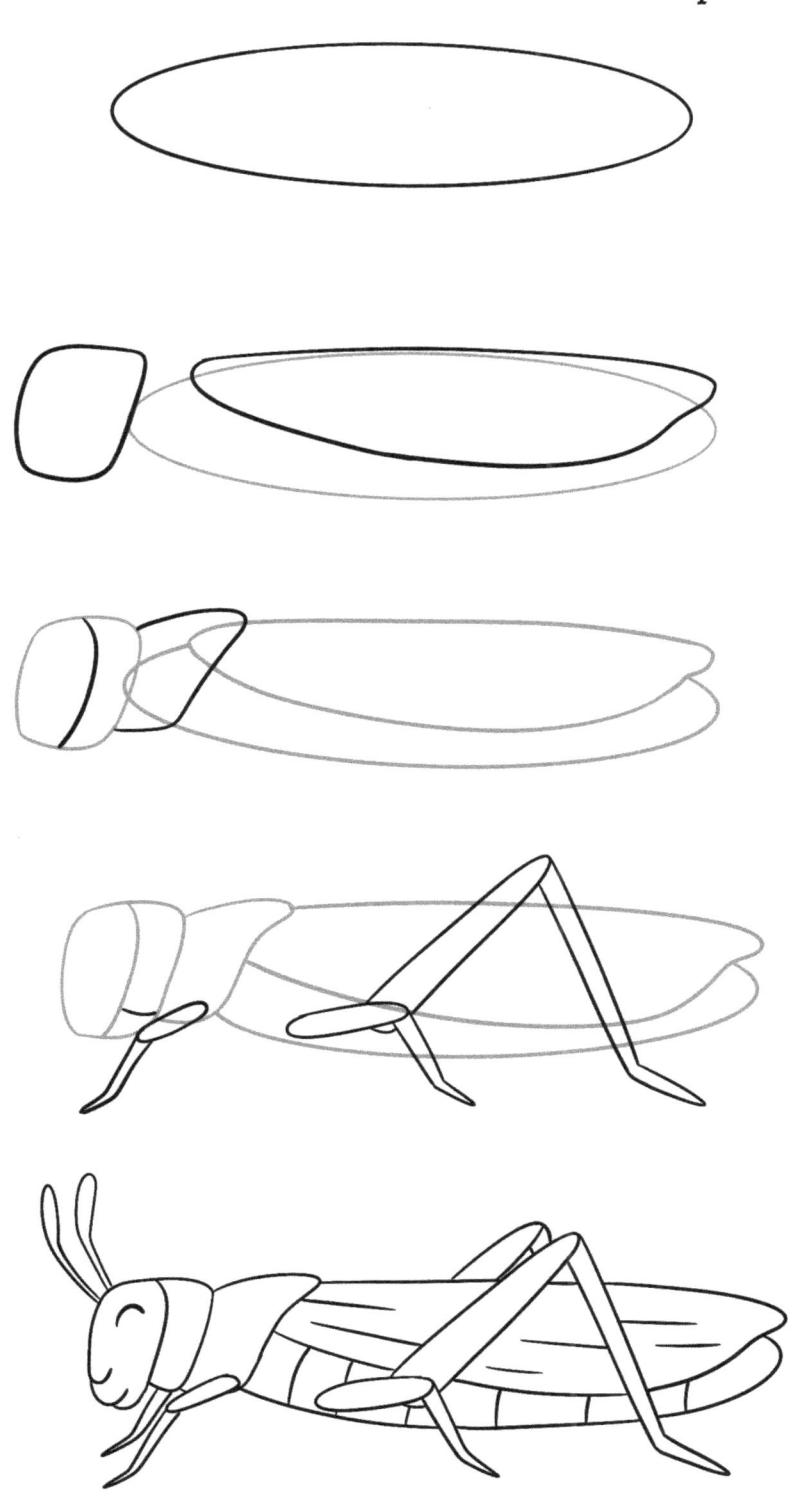

Color and count the moths in the garden scene

*Moths are excellent at camouflage and can mimic shapes like leaves and bark.

Find the 2 Quails that are identical

*Quail are ground-nesting birds; they typically lay their eggs in shallow scrapes on the ground often hidden in tall grass or under bushes.

*Only female mosquitoes bite; they need the protein in blood to develop their eggs while males feed on nectar and other plant juices.

Word Search

```
S  I  F  T  R  G  S  N  A  K  E  F
C  T  A  B  N  B  O  U  A  F  L  Y
A  C  H  M  R  I  L  T  T  E  L  L
T  H  G  N  X  T  P  O  Z  I  C  S
E  C  S  S  I  E  T  H  O  R  N  K
M  O  S  Q  U  I  T  O  G  D  N  Y
```

- BITE
- MOSQUITO
- BLOOD
- FLY
- TINY
- ITCH

What is your favorite animal from the Quran? Draw and explain▽

_____
_____
_____
_____

www.ingramcontent.com/pod-product-compliance
Lightning Source LLC
LaVergne TN
LVHW070838080426
835510LV00030B/3444